U.S. VIRGIN IS

ST. THOMAS · ST. JOHN · ST. CROIX

Photos by
Andrea Pistolesi

BONECHI

© Copyright 1994 by Casa Editrice Bonechi, via Cairoli 18/b - 50131 Florence - Italy
Tel. 55/576841 - Telex 571323 CEB - Fax 55/5000766
Printed in Italy by Centro Stampa Editoriale Bonechi.
Photographs from the archives of Casa Editrice Bonechi taken by ANDREA PISTOLESI *with the exception of photograph on page 78 taken by* G. Bausi, Agenzia K & B News, Florence.
The photo on page 75 is a courtesy of Mario Bojola.
Text by KATE PARENTI

ISBN 88-8029-177-7

★   ★   ★

INTRODUCTION

The United States Virgin Islands are part of the semi-circular arc of islands which starts south-east of the Florida Keys and extends as far as Trinidad off the North East coast of South America, dividing the tropical waters of the Caribbean Sea from the Atlantic Ocean. They are situated approximately 40 miles east of Puerto Rico, and are the first link in the chain known as the Leeward Islands of the Lesser Antilles which makes up the north-east boundary of the Caribbean. St. Croix's Point Udall is the easternmost point of land in the United States. St. John (20 sq. miles, population 3,504 in 1990 census) and St. Thomas (32 sq. miles, population 48,166) are volcanic in origin which gives them the appearance, seen along with the nearby British Virgin Islands just east of St. John over the Sir Francis Drake Channel, of a partially submerged mountain range: steep hills and deeply indented bays surrounded by dozens of smaller islets and cays. St. Croix (84 sq. miles) lies approximately 35 miles to the south of the other two, and is not volcanic, with rolling hills in the northwest which slope down to a coastal plain, and long straight shorelines with few sheltered bays. The group of islands was discovered by Columbus during his second voyage in 1493. He claimed the land for Spain and named it "Las Once Mil Viogenes" (the 11,000 virgins), supposedly reminded of St. Ursula's legendary companions by the profusion of peaks. Columbus stopped first at St. Croix, naming it Santa Cruz, and sent his men ashore to look for fresh water; they were, however, soon driven off by the natives, fierce Carib Indians. For the next hundred years, the Spanish showed very little interest in the islands, apart from raiding them to carry off the natives to work in the gold mines of Santo Domingo. In fact, when European settlers arrived, after the defeat of the Spanish Armada, there were no native Indians left on the islands. The islands were, however, much used by pirates and privateers to hide their ships and their booty and to lie in wait for the treasure-laden Spanish galleons. The seventeenth century was more stormy with the British, French, Spanish, Dutch and Danish battling to possess these islands which were on the trade route of sailing ships bound from Europe to the Americas. A certain stability arrived when St. Thomas was possessed in the name of Denmark in 1666; St. John followed in 1684, though it was not colonized until 1716. St. Croix, after a violent early history being fought over by the Dutch, the English, the Spanish and the French, and a period under the Knights of Malta, was bought by the Danish West India and Guinea Company from France in 1733. The three islands became a Danish Crown Colony in 1755 and the King of Denmark made them free ports in 1764. For a long time the islands thrived: St. Thomas was a major port for trans-shipment and trade and there were sugar and cotton plantations on all the islands. In particular, the large flat plains at the centre of St. Croix proved ideal for the production of sugar cane: at the peak of its productivity this island was one of the richest sugar islands in the Caribbean, with hundreds of working plantations. Sugar, rum and the slave trade flourished until the banning of the slave trade at the end of the eighteenth century by Denmark, and the abolition of slavery in 1848 which created a difficult labour situation. This along with other factors sent the islands into a steady decline: landowners gave up and let their fields go into grass, putting in herds of cattle; between 1850 and 1930 the population dwindled by half leaving mostly the descendants of slaves. In 1917, the United States, concerned to protect its interests in the Panama Canal, and seeing the strategic importance of the islands which are very near the major shipping lanes to the Canal, bought the islands for $25 million as a naval base. The Danish West Indies became the United States Virgin Islands. For the next fourteen years the U.S. Navy was in charge of the islands and their economy sunk still lower; even the last rum distilleries were closed under National Prohibition. When President Hoover visited the islands shortly after, he described them as an "effective poorhouse". In 1931 the Department of The Interior replaced the U.S. Navy as the bureaucracy in charge of the territory and the area now has a governor, elected every 2 years, and a senate of 15 members. The economy picked up after the 1950s with the ever growing influx of tourists. The islands enjoy a pleasant sub-tropical climate with temperatures which vary only a few degrees during the year, averaging an all round temperature of 26°C. Even the hottest summer day however is cooled by the trade winds blowing from the east. The surface temperature of the water is little different from that of the air: 25-30°C. This climate, along with the crystal-clear waters full of marine life, coral reefs and sunken ships to explore, make the Virgin Islands a paradise for sunbathing, snorkelling, scuba-diving and, of course, sailing.

Fauna

The most common fauna, to the point of becoming a pest, is the prolific mongoose which was imported during the plantation era to rid the islands of cane rats. It had no effect on the rats, but is probably the reason why there are no snakes on the islands. There are many species of birds: pelicans diving for fish are a common sight and the little bananaquit bird which feeds on fruit, nectar and small insects can often be seen on outdoor tables searching for something sweet, hence its other name, the sugar bird.

Vegetation on the islands is very varied, though

The fauna of these islands is rich and varied, particularly the bird species and, of course, that to be seen in the marvellous undersea world.

Flora

...uch of it is second growth as most of the land was ...eared years ago for sugar and cotton cultivation. ...ome areas are arid, particularly the east end of St. ...roix, with grassland and several species of cactus, ...thers abound in flamboyant tropical growth with ...owering bushes, fruit trees and palms; on St. Croix ...ere is even a rain forest. Along the sea shore can ...e found sea-grapes, palms and manchineels, the ...poison apple tree" which is usually labelled ...arning people not to eat the fruit. The most ...ommon flowering plants are bougainvillea ...brought to the West Indies in the 1700s by the ...ench navigator Bougainville), hibiscus, frangi-...ani, orchids, oleanders and poinsettias. Fruit trees ...clude pineapple, papaya, mango, citrus fruits, ...readfruit, banana and coconut.
...order to find out more about the flora ...n each of the islands, on St. Thomas ...ere is an arboretum behind Magens Bay ...each and a Botanical Garden at the ...ouffer Grand Beach Resort which offers ...guided tour, the National Park of St. John ...fers nature treks, and St. Croix has the ...George Village Botanical Garden.

The Caribbean flora is rich in species: hundreds of different plants are to be found and wonderfully coloured flowers which are sometimes very poisonous.

Aerial view of St. Thomas Harbour with cruise ships at the West India Company Dock.

Aerial view of old town centre with Legislature building and King Wharf in the foreground; behind them is Fort Christian.

ST. THOMAS

St. Thomas is the middle sized United States Virgin Island: 14 miles long and about 3, often mountainous, miles across (Crown Mountain on this island is 1,556 m. high; the highest in the U.S. Virgin Islands). It is the most accessible and the most densely populated. Its natural deep water harbour makes it a favoured stop over for Caribbean cruise liners and it also has an international airport. Its chief town, Charlotte Amalie, is the capital of the U.S. Virgin Islands and the most lively in commercial terms: duty free shopping is one of its main attractions and it boasts an active and cosmopolitan night life with no lack of night clubs and good restaurants. St. Thomas was uncolonised until 1672, though much used by pirates intent on plundering treasure-laden Spanish ships. The first settlers arrived on May 23rd 1672 on behalf of the Danish West India and Guinea Company with a charter from King Christian V, after whose wife Charlotte Amalie they named their harbour settlement.

Being mountainous, and thus somewhat handicapped for agriculture, St. Thomas conveniently positioned and with a large safe harbour soon began prospering as the main West Indian trading station. As Denmark remained a neutral nation in the constant wars of Europe, it threw its chief West Indian port open to all, including privateers and pirates who brought trade to the island, furnishing commodities at easy rates and buying the provisions produced by the planters. Commerce was further boosted in 1724 when St. Thomas was proclaimed a free port which it remains today. Soon after the colony was established, the first slave ships from Africa arrived in the harbour and St. Thomas became a point in the famous trade triangle: sugar, molasses, cotton and indigo were shipped to Britain's North American colonies, from there goods such as textiles, iron, guns and alcohol were transported to North West Africa. These wares were traded for captives who were loaded for the return voyage to the Caribbean and sold in the slave markets.

Today the warehouses running from Dronningens Gade (pronounced ga-da), the main street, to the sea front still illustrate the importance of trade to this island: teeming with tourists, they now house shops full of tax-free luxury goods: cameras, perfumes, cosmetics, jewelry, alcohol. However, this is by no means all the island has to offer; it has more than 40 beaches, among which is the famous beach of Magens Bay, rated among the 10 most beautiful beaches in the world.

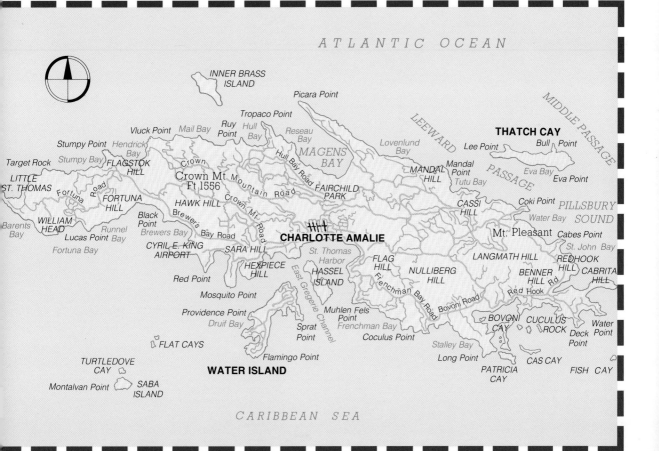

Panoramic view of St. Thomas Harbour and Charlotte Amalie

CHARLOTTE AMALIE

The capital of the U.S. Virgin Islands, **Charlotte Amalie** has always been the hub of St. Thomas life with most of the island's population concentrated here. Much of the town's historic centre is Danish and it retains the character of an eighteenth century Caribbean port with winding lanes and narrow streets, some so steep that they turn into flights of steps and solid old colonial warehouses that are now transformed inside into elegant shops.

Charlotte Amalie was one of the most important trading and trans-shipment ports of the West Indies for more than 200 years and thus the deepwater harbour has always been the heart of the city. The harbour shoreline itself can tell us much about the history of Charlotte Amalie, the places of interest and its more recent attractions. Starting at the very westernmost tip, **Cowell's Point** marks a short English tenure; fortifications and historical maritime buildings can be visited. The land on which it stands now known as **Hassel Island**, was once part of St. Thomas itself but was separated in order to provide an escape route for the U.S. Navy. Across this narrow channel lies **French town**, the picturesque home of the fishing contingent of French settlers who fled the

island of St. Barthélemy after it became Swedish towards the end of the eighteenth century. They have retained their French-Norman dialect and culture: some good French restaurants are to be found in the neighbourhood.

The historical centre of Charlotte Amalie lies more or less between French town and Frederiksberg Point, on the hill above which stands Bluebeard's Castle. In the centre stands the red building of Fort Christian set slightly back, with the lime green building of the Legislature in front and the coast guard dock nearby.

The old docks were west of Fort Christian and until the new dual-lane highway was built along the waterfront, the original railway tracks which carried merchandise in trolleys along the grid pattern of alleyways leading to Dronningens Gade still reached the sea front.

East of Bluebeard's Hill lies the **Yacht Haven Marina**, one of the largest and most complete yachting service facilities in the Caribbean. Ending the harbour's shoreline is the 2,334 foot pier of the **West India Company dock**, capable of berthing four cruise ships.

Aerial view of Bluebeard's Hill and Castle.

Bluebeard's Castle

BLUEBEARD'S CASTLE

Bluebeard's Castle is a round stone tower of brick and rubble masonry standing at the top of Frederiksberg, an imposing hill overlooking the old centre of Charlotte Amalie and St. Thomas harbour from the east. It is one of the earliest fortifications on St. Thomas and was formerly called Frederiksfort. The Danish government built it as a coast defense installation in the second half of the seventeenth century and until 1735 Danish troops used it as a fort and look out and manned the 11 cannon.

According to legend, the tower was the seat of Bluebeard the Pirate who committed horrible crimes there. This legend probably originated from the real presence of pirates and privateers on this island due to the town's policy of tolerance: privateers were allowed to use the harbour for as long as they liked, pirates could use it but had to leave within 24 hours. The difference between the two was simple: a pirate robbed ship and crew then killed the men and a privateer took ship and cargo, robbed the men, but spared their lives. They were tolerated and even in certain periods and under certain governors, encouraged because they were good for trade, providing merchandise at good prices and buying their provisions from the planters.

Today Bluebeard's Castle is surrounded by a luxury resort of the same name. The hotel was first opened in 1934 and now has 170 rooms with all modern conveniences, a swimming pool, tennis courts, a cocktail lounge and a couple of restaurants, all on th landscape garden hillside. The old tower houses Victorian-style honeymoon suites.

The Legislature building.

The entrance to the Legislature building.

THE LEGISLATURE BUILDING

This stately lime-green building just beyond the
Coast Guard headquarters at King's Wharf was buil
in the second half of the nineteenth century as a
Danish Marine barracks. Completed around 1879, i
is now forum for the legislature of the 15 elected
senators. The cerimony transferring the islands to th
United States took place in front of this building on
Saturday, March 31st, 1917. Initially the islands wer
governed by the U.S. Navy, then in 1936 an Organic
Act was passed by the U.S. Congress granting civil
government by presidentially appointed governors
In 1954 a Revised Organic Act was passed by
Congress which provided for the legislature and
separate executive, legislative and judicial branche
and in 1970 Congress granted islanders the right to
elect their own governor; in 1972, their own
congressional delegate. The Governor is elected
every four years and the 15 Senators who handle
local affairs are elected every 2 years. Judicial pow
is vested in local courts and district courts. To the
east along the harbour front just beyond the
Legislature building are the police department and
the Federal building.

FORT CHRISTIAN

On the façade of what is probably the oldest standing building in the U.S. Virgin Islands 1671, the presumed date of construction, can be read. The actual date is uncertain and the building has been constantly repaired and rebuilt over the years after suffering damage from hurricanes, earthquakes, fire and bombardment. The name Fort Christian was given in honour of King Christian V.

In the past the fort has served as governor's residence, church, townhall, police station and jail; it is now the home of the Virgin Islands Museum. The former cells which once held planters who were unable to pay their taxes can be visited and museum exhibits include Carib and Arawak Indian remains and stone-age Indian tools. There is also an exhibition of life in the Danish West Indies with displays illustrating the European settlement, the prosperity era, the Decline and Stagnation era and harbour scenes from 1941 - 1950. Also on show are old navigational charts, African ornaments and a collection of rare Caribbean seahells.

Aerial view of Fort Christian and the Legislature.

The clock tower of Fort Christian.

Next page, a view of Government Hill from the harbour.

THE FREEDOM BELL AND BUST OF CHRISTIAN V IN EMANCIPATION PARI

Emancipation Park is a charming garden at the ea end of Main Street which commemorates the Danis Governor Peter von Scholten's proclamation on the 3rd of July 1848 (some 15 years prior to Lincoln's proclamation in the United States) freeing all slaves The two statues in the park link the islands past: a bronze bust of King Christian V of Denmark and in the south-west corner, a scaled down replica of Philadelphia's Liberty Bell. Overlooking the park is stately example of old West Indian architecture, the former **Grand Hotel**, the third storey of which blew off many years ago in a hurricane. The park itself is the site of many of St. Thomas' official ceremonies.

A scaled-down replica of Philadelphia's Liberty Bell.

Bronze bust of King Christian V of Denmark.

FØDT 8 APRIL 1818

KONGE 15 NOVEMBER 1863

DØD 29 JANUAR 1906

Façade of Frederick Lutheran Church.

Windows of Frederick Lutheran Church.

HE FREDERICK LUTHERAN CHURCH

earby on Norre Gade, no.7, is the present
rederick Lutheran Evangelical Church which was
arted in 1789 and completed in 1793, but was
tered extensively after being gutted by fire in 1829.
ther churches had existed before this one as
utheranism had been the established Danish
ligion since 1536. This is a Gothic revival building
proached by a wide staircase, with a projecting
ntral entrance pavillion, round-arched door and
ell-tower. Inside it is decorated with antique
andeliers and has a collection of eighteenth
entury Danish ecclesiastical silver and a 1783 gold
alice.

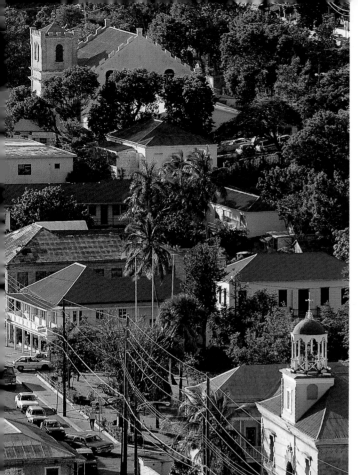

THE MORAVIAN MEMORIAL CHURCH

Further east on the same street as the Frederick Lutheran Church is the **Moravian Memorial Church**. It was constructed in 1844 to commemorate the 25th anniversary of Moravian presence on the island. Outside it has rusticated quoins and window and door surrounds and a little wooden cupola; inside it is cool and white with graceful columns which support balconies. The Moravian Bretheren are a Christian Protestant sect and their church was founded in Bohemia in 1457. They were driven out o Bohemia in 1722 after long persecution.

View of Norre Gade with Moravian Church on the right in the foreground and Frederick Lutheran Church in the background.

Moravian Memorial Church.

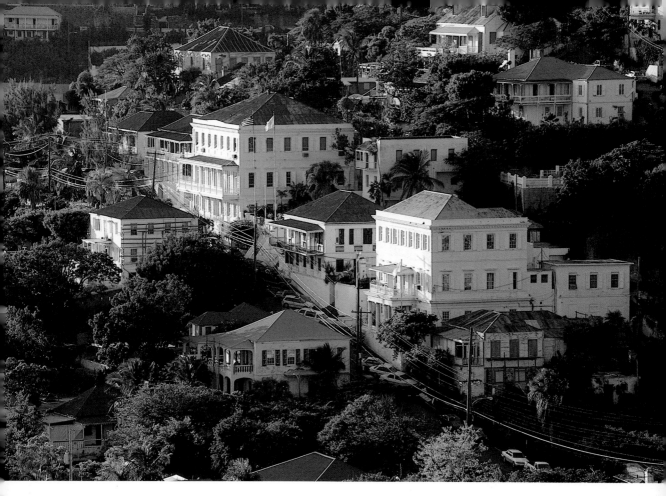

Government Hill, with Government House on the left, and lower Town on the right, the Lieutenant Governor's Office.

GOVERNMENT HOUSE

Government House is a gracious three-story brick edifice with long balconies in wrought iron situated in **Government Hill** to the left at the bottom of the 99 steps. The style of this building, constructed between 865-7 as a meeting place for the Danish Colonial Council is typical of old houses and public buildings throughout the West Indies. It is now the official residence and office of the elected Governor of the U.S. Virgin Islands. At the foot of the ceremonial stairs stands an authentic Danish guardhouse like those used by sentries in public places in Denmark; it was presented to Government House in 1967 on the occasion of the 50th anniversary of the day that the Virgin Islands were tranferred from Danish to United States ownership.

Part of the house, including the second floor reception/ballroom with balcony, can be visited. There are frescoes showing various important moments in the history of the Virgin Islands and a collection of oil paintings by artists from St. Thomas, the most prominent being Camille Pissarro, the famous Impressionist painter, friend and teacher of Cézanne and Gauguin, who was born on St. Thomas

19

The Lieutenant Governor's Office.

Government Hou

Detail of the wrought iron balcony at Government House.

in 1830, of a Jewish father and a Creole mother. Before going to Paris he worked in his father's shop in Dronningens Gade and lived above it. His paren are buried in the Jewish cemetery west of the city. Another interesting house on Government Hill is **Crown House** which was built as a private house in 1750. It served as the Danish governor of the island residence for many years. It is located at the top of the 99 steps.

Blackbeard's Castle

BLACKBEARD'S CASTLE

Situated at the top of the 99 steps on Blackbeard's Hill, this stone tower was built by Governor Jorge Iversen after the French attack on St. Thomas in February 1678 and was originally known as Fort Skytsborg. According to legend, it was the haunt the celebrated pirate Blackbeard, Edward Teach Bristol, England who was disposed of by the Britis navy in 1718.
Blackbeard's Castle is now a small exclusive res with a famous restaurant, dominated by the 300 year-old tower.

MARK ST. THOMAS HOTEL

Near Blackbeard's Castle, also at the top of the 99 steps is the **Mark St. Thomas Hotel**, a restored two-story brick mansion built in 1785 and standing high above the harbour. It is one of the most frequently recommended places in town for dining and accomodation and each of its 9 rooms is decorated with antiques and period reproductions. The dining room and veranda have splendid views over the harbour.

The Mark St. Thomas Hotel.

View over the harbour from the balcony of the Mark St. Thomas Hotel.

THE 99 STEPS AND HOTEL 1829

Between Hotel 1829 and Government House the **99 steps** climb from Government Hill to Lille Tarne Gade (Danish for Little Tower Street). In actual fact not 99, but 103, this step-street was one of many bui? by the Danes to solve the problem of getting up and down the town's steep hills. It dates back to the 1700s.

Hotel 1829 was formerly called Lavalette House and was built by a French sea captain, Lavalette, for his bride (his initials appear in the wrought iron of the balcony); it was finished in 1829. Now this pink building with green awnings is a hotel with large air guest rooms, a shady terrace for afternoon reading and a beautiful sunny courtyard with a pool.

The 99 Steps.

Hotel 1829 as seen from Dronningens Gade.

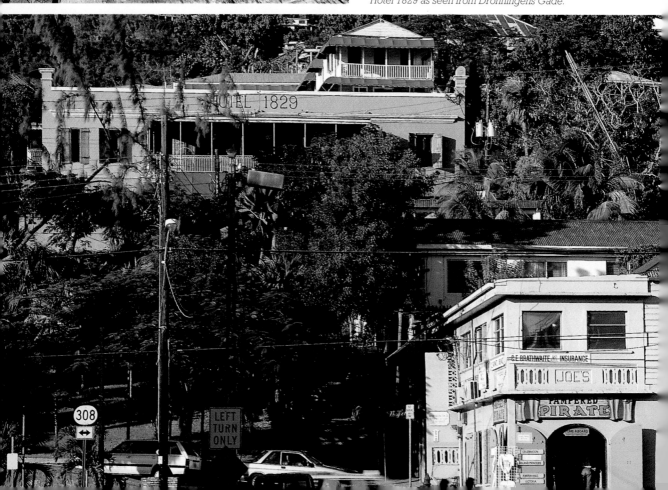

Converted warehouses housing elegant shops on Dronningens Gade.

MAIN STREET
OR DRONNINGENS GADE

Main Street is still officially known by its Danish name **Dronningens Gade**. The street is largely made up of old colonial warehouses with vaulted arches, arched doorways and heavy shutters; they were built of thick masonry after the original wooden ones succumbed to fire and hurricanes. Lanes lead from Dronningens Gade to the waterfront and before the dual-lane road along the sea front was built, these lanes and alleys had railway tracks for transporting merchandise. This was the old docks warehouse area when Charlotte Amalie was the main port for cargo trans-shipment in the Caribbean, all merchandise was unloaded and loaded, stored, sold and consigned here; the slave market was in the market place at the west end of Dronningens Gade. Now, because of St. Thomas' freeport status, this area is dubbed "the shopping Mecca of the Caribbean" and tourists flock to Main Street to purchase luxury goods at bargain prices: precious jewelry, watches, cameras, designer clothing, perfume, leather goods, china, crystal, and liquor. The present rules for U.S. citizens allow up to $1,200 worth of duty free goods per person including children, every 30 days. In addition, one duty free gift a day valued up to $100 may be sent to a friend or relative. Also any U.S. residents over 21 may take back 5 fifths of liquor and a 6th if it is produced in the Virgin Islands.

Although most of the buildings on Dronningens Gade were warehouses, there are also a few old iron-balconied residences; in one of these, 14 Dronningens Gade, Camille Pissarro (1830-1903) was born. The Camille Pissarro Art Gallery is now based on the first floor here and not only sells Impressionist prints and gifts, but also has a fine collection of original art by a variety of local and regional artists.

Parallel to Dronningens Gade, behind it, is

A typical mall, one of the main attractions for tourists.

Crystal Gade.

A typical tourist bus, locally known as a Safari bus, on Dronningens Gade.

(left) Palm Passage.

(right) Riise's Alley.

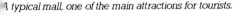
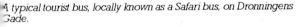

Wimmelskafts Gade, a narrow lane crowded with many of St. Thomas' clubs and pubs.

The **market place** located at the west end of Dronningens Gade was the site of one of the busiest slave markets of the eighteenth century. St. Thomas was a point in the lucrative slave trade triangle which had its peak from 1740-1810 with the demand for labour on plantations: European and New England merchants transported manufactured goods such as textiles, guns, liquor and iron to North West Africa. Trading their wares for people, they transported the slaves across the Atlantic, a dreaded 2 month long voyage which came to be called the " middle passage". The slaves were stored in inhuman conditions on wooden platforms, some only able to crouch, some forced to lie down. So many died that some times a ship load was purchased with a specified minimum survival number. The captives were exchanged in the Carribean for sugar, molasses, rum, cotton and indigo. St. Thomas itself produced sugar which was shipped raw to Copenhagen, where sugar processing was for a time the main industry.

The present iron roof over this open structure was bought from a European railway company in the early 1900s. The market is now a produce market where islanders buy and sell local fruit and vegetables. It is open every day except Sunday and is most lively in the early morning. Sometimes it is also possible to buy local produce, particularly coconuts, on the waterfront, going straight down Strand Gade from Market Square, where they are sold off boats.

Parallel to Strand Gade, running between the water front and Dronningens Gade are many little narrow streets and alleyways in a grid pattern. These lanes were lined with warehouses and the rails on which trolleys for transporting merchandise between the ships and the warehouses ran can still be seen in some of them. The rails originally reached the waterfront until the new dual-lane waterfront highway was built.

THE SEPHARDIC SYNAGOGUE

The **Sephardic Synagogue** of Beracha Veshalom Vegemiluth Hasidim ("Blessing and Peace and Acts of Piety") is on Crystal Gade and can be reached from Main Street by a steep climb up Raadet's Gade. The congregation was founded in 1796 when the first synagogue was constructed, but there is documentary evidence of Jews living on St. Thomas from 1665. In 1801 only 9 families belonged to the congregation, but by 1824 there were 64. Replaced twice, the present building was completed in 1833 and given its present name. This synagogue is the second oldest synagogue in the Western Hemisphere. The interior is very impressive with a domed ceiling supported by four Ionic columns, original nineteenth century lighting fixtures and a four-sided tiered seating arrangement of mahogany pews. The sand covering the floor commemorates the biblical exodus of the Jews from Egypt over the desert.

A characteristic sloping street.

The Sephardic Synagogue

Interior of Sephardic Synagogue

Following pages, Charlotte Amalie at night.

Denmark Hill with the Danish consulate at the top, flying the "Dannebrog", the Danish flag along with the Stars and Stripes.

*erial view of Muhlenfels Pt. and the Frenchman's Reef Hotel;
:hind it can be seen St. Thomas Harbour.*

Frenchman's Reef Hotel and Morningstar Beach.

RENCHMAN'S REEF HOTEL AND :ORNINGSTAR BEACH

le huge **Frenchman's Reef Hotel** stands on the
:omontory which is the easternmost point of St.
iomas' harbour, three sides of it facing the sea. On
e other side of the promontory is Morningstar
each, the first large beach east of the Charlotte
nalie harbour. Between the hotel and its luxury
:sort on the beach, the **Morningstar Beach Club**,
ere are 520 rooms, all overlooking the sea. The
tel complex, the biggest in the U.S. Virgin Islands
s 6 restaurants, 2 pools, 4 tennis courts available
y and night and over 20 duty-free shops. A water
xi service to Charlotte Amalie operates from the
tel and there is a cliff-front elevator to reach
orningstar beach, which is a lively place and
pular with local residents. The 96 luxury rooms of
e Morningstar Beach Club are situated in 5

structures on the beach; they are furnished in
tropical style and all have a balcony and private
entrance.
The Virgin Islands are blessed with wonderful
conditions for the practice of water sports: constant
trade winds, warm sea, countless calm bays in which
to drop anchor, coral reefs and sunken ships to
explore, fine sports fishing (the World Record Blue
Marlin was caught in these waters in 1977; it held the
record until 1992 and is now on display at the Cyril
E. King Airport). Frenchman's Reef Hotel has the
largest centre for water sports on the island offering
scuba, snorkelling, watersport equipment rental,
yacht cruises, small sailboat rentals and lessons,
sailing, wind-surfing, parasailing and deep sea
fishing. Some good·snorkelling can be had in the
bay: at the east end are stands of elkhorn and brain
coral with plenty of colourful tropical fish darting in
and out between them. Nearby are various dive sites
including the navy wrecks and Armando's Reef.

View of Magens Bay from Drake's Seat.　　　　　　　　　　　　　　　*Aerial view of Magens Bay.*

MAGENS BAY

From **Mountain Top** (nearly 1,500 ft high) a spectacular panoramic view can be had of **Magens Bay**, the U.S. cays and smaller islands beyond it, and beyond them, the British Virgins. Another slightly lower vantage point from which to view the most famous and largest beach of St. Thomas is **Drake's Seat**. According to legend, it was from here that Sir Francis Drake, Elizabethan pirate and explorer, inveterate plunderer of treasure-laden Spanish ships, surveyed the fleet that he had assembled to attack Puerto Rico.
Drake's Seat was established by Mr. Arthur S. Fairchild, a wealthy American publishing tycoon, who bought the Louisenhoj estate on which it is situated, land and buildings, early this century (the old gatehouse is visible at the top of the hill before turning down towards the Bay). Luckily for St. Thomas dwellers, Magens Bay was also part of this property and he deeded it and the land surrounding it to the people of the Virgin Islands "in perpetuity without regard to race or colour"; for this reason it

has remained unspoilt and undeveloped. Magens Bay, which is rated among the 10 most beautiful beaches in the World, is nearly 3/4 mile of fine white coral sand so well protected by long peninsulas on either side that the water is always calm. The beach slopes back to rows of sea grape with its thick, rounded leaves and large drooping clusters of grape-like fruit (from which an excellent jam can be made) and haiti-haiti trees. Behind these is a plantation of tall graceful coconut palms, the fruit of which can be purchased green from roadside vendors for the coconut water. When ripe, the coconut can be eaten as it is or can be used to make coconut milk, much used in island cooking. Fairchild preserved the salt pond and the mangroves behind the beach which are so important for the ecosystem, and behind the beach at the western end he planted an **Arboretum** with both imported and indigenous trees, many of which are labelled. Nearby there are some Danish sugar mill ruins; all can be visited.

Aerial view of the Coral World Complex.

The Coral World Underwater Observatory.

CORAL WORLD

Coral World Marine Park, a 4.5 acre park on the north-east side of the island, opened in December 1977. The big attraction here is the three-floor underwater observatory, one of only three in the world, sunk in a coral reef and giving visitors a 20 ft.-below-the-sea divers-view of coral formations, sponges, tropical fish giant anemones and other marine life. Windows completely encircle both underwater levels giving a 360° view and on the walls informative plaques help identify the more common species.

The underwater observatory is also open 3 nights a week for those interested to see the exciting and quite different night marine life.
Under the other domes at Coral World are an 80,000 gallon aquarium, the Marine Garden Aquarium with sea stars and living coral and the Predator Tank containing sharks and moray eels; new acquisitions are two Sea World Explorers which simulate the experience of going in a submarine. There is also a restaurant/bar with a sea view and a few shops selling ocean-related gifts.

Underwater round St. Thomas

Coral World is an interesting and informative way to see a coral reef and some of the colourful tropical fish which live there, but the curiosity of a large number of people does not stop here: government research has discovered that over a quarter of all visitors to the U.S. Virgin Islands spend a part of their time snorkelling and/or scuba diving. Thus, over the years, thanks to the abundance and variety of interesting sites it has to offer and the consistent good visibility, St. Thomas has developed into one of the top diving centres in the Caribbean.

For divers, great variety is available: new wrecks, old wrecks, caves, tunnels, ledges, reefs; Pillsbury Sound, the passage between St. Thomas and St. John is full of small islands, cays and pinnacles with interesting dives everywhere, most requiring only a 10-30 min. boat trip. Near St. Thomas popular wrecks are the *Cartarser Senior,* the *General Rogers,* which was a Coast Guard buoy purposely sunk to create a fish habitat, and the *West Indies Trader* at

Witshoal, a 400 ft. freighter upright on a sand
bottom at 40 ft. These wrecks are covered in
different kinds of coral and are habitats for many
species of tropical fish (200 species of marine
fish in the Caribbean are known).
For non-scuba divers good snorkelling is
possible from many beaches, but another way of
visiting the coral reefs round St. Thomas is in the
Atlantis, an electrically-powered submarine
which holds 46 passengers. The submarine
descends to 90 feet in its one-hour tours and also
offers night dives. It leaves from the cruise ship
dock.

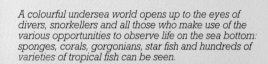

*A colourful undersea world opens up to the eyes of
divers, snorkellers and all those who make use of the
various opportunities to observe life on the sea bottom:
sponges, corals, gorgonians, star fish and hundreds of
varieties of tropical fish can be seen.*

COKI BEACH

Nearby Coral World is **Coki Beach**, one of the most popular beaches on St. Thomas and the best for scuba diving and snorkelling, especially at night. There are shallow reefs teeming with fish at both the east and west ends of the beach and there is also a drop off in the channel.

The off-shore island facing Coki Beach is **Thatch Cay** which has a series of underwater tunnels suitable for certified divers. The island is thought to have been named after the pirate Edward Teach, or Thatch, called Blackbeard. who, according to legend, burie his treasure here on the beach.

Near Coki beach at Tutu is **Jim Tillet's Silk Screening Studio** where not only this artist's work can be seen, but also collections of paintings and sculptures by local artists. Three times a year well attended Arts and Crafts Fairs are held here.

p, left, aerial view with Great Bay on the right with long, narrow
ssup Bay and Red Hook ferry point behind it. The bay on the left
Cowpet Bay and Jersey Bay lies beyond it.

tom, left, aerial view with Cabes point in the foreground, part of
ith Bay to the right, St.John's Bay after Cabes Point with the
phire Beach Resort (grey rectangular blocks) just before
ttyklip Point and the marina just beyond it. The little rounded hill
Redhook Hill.

Aerial view of Mahogany Run golf course.

*Following pages, sunset over St. Thomas and coconut palms
and a travellers' palm.*

THE EASTERN TIP OF ST. THOMAS

e eastern tip of St. Thomas is blessed with many
autiful beaches and as a result there is a fair
ount of development for tourism with resorts,
ndominiums and large hotels. The natural centre
the eastern tip is **Red Hook**, an important town for
ating and sportsfishing with an hourly ferry
vice to St. John and, less frequently, for the British
gin Islands, Jost Van Dyke and Virgin Gorda.
hting facilities are also very good here: in long,
rrow Vessup Bay which leads into the ferry docks
Redhook the **American Yacht Harbour** is to be
nd, from here yachts can also be chartered; also
famous **Sapphire Beach Resort** from which the
ach nearby takes its name has its own marina,
ering the usual services. For sportsfishing, the **St.
omas Sport Fishing Centre** is based next to the
ry dock.
mous beaches, following the coastline, are

Sapphire Beach, Vessup Beach, Muller Bay (a series
of beaches which stretch from Vessup Beach almost
as far as Cabrita Point); Great Bay (with its new and
beautiful Grand Palazzo Hotel which opened in
August 1992), and Cowpet Bay, where the St.
Thomas Yacht Club is located. A large proportion of
this beach is bordered by the Cowpet Bay
Condominium, one of the oldest and best
established of developments on the island.
Inland, on the east end of St. Thomas is the
Mahogany Run championship 18-hole golf course
which was designed by George and Tom Fazio.
The course stretches 6,525 yards and has the 13th
and 14th green situated near dramatic cliffs
overlooking the Atlantic Ocean.
Mahogany Run also offers a golf clubhouse, a fully-
equipped pro shop, a driving range and a practice
putting green.

ST. JOHN

St. John is the smallest of the three major U.S. Virgin Islands being approximately 20 square miles; it is the least populated and the least commercially developed. It lies about 3 miles east of St. Thomas across the Pillsbury Sound. Large scale agriculture was abandoned here over 250 years ago and the island has been protected from commercial development by the generosity of Laurance S. Rockefeller who, wishing to protect its natural beauty bought land here in the 1950s and donated it to establish the Virgin Islands National Park which is now 74% of the island's area.

St. John was originally inhabited by Indians, traces of whose settlements have been found all along the island's north shore. It was formally taken possession of by the Danes in 1684, but was was not colonised until 1716 when the Danish West India and Guinea Company established its large Estate Carolina on Coral Bay.

By 1733 the whole land mass was divided into 109 estates and the steep hillsides were cleared and terraced and planted with cotton and sugar cane. The population was 2,402, little more than 200 of whom were white. Then, after a particularly difficult summer with drought, a plague of insects and a hurricane, the first major black rebellion of the Caribbean broke out. On November 13th 1733, a group of slaves entered Berg Fort at Coral Bay with bundles of firewood in which knives were hidden. They slaughtered the soldiers and fired two shots, the signal to the other rebels to massacre all whites and burn the great houses and mills. The rebels held the island for six months, but were eventually overcome and surrounded at St. Mary's Point near the Annaberg estate buildings, where, seeing no way of escaping they committed suicide rather than surrender. Strangely, after this the island never really recovered: the Danes started to cultivate St. Croix which they bought in 1733 instead and St. John was left very much to itself, thus remaining undeveloped and quiet. Now, in addition to its 33 beautiful unspoilt beaches, a great attraction is the National Park itself where a large part of the island can be seen on foot, by following the many trails through park land.

...nset over Cruz Bay Harbour.

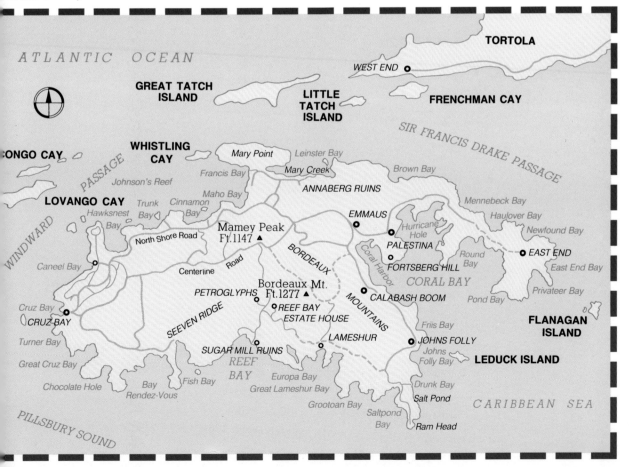

View of Gallows Point Suite Resort from the harbour.

View of Cruz Bay with harbour, ferry dock, red-roofed Battery ar Gallows Point Suite Reso

Pages 52-53, aerial view of Cruz Bay with Large Por visible on the rig

CRUZ BAY

Cruz Bay is the main settlement and the point of entry to St. John, either by ferry from Red Hook or Charlotte Amalie on St. Thomas or by sea plane from Christiansted, St. Croix. The town is small and relaxed and offers the basics: car rental, shops, restaurants, watersports and boating facilities. There is a small amount of history in the form of the **Battery**, built in 1735 to protect the island and the **Elaine Lone Sprauve Museum**, a former Enighed great house with exhibits including remains from pre-Columbian days and Danish West Indies history and artifacts, as well as information on marine life and frequent community art exhibitions.

The **National Park U.S. Ranger Station** is also based here on the waterfront. It organises guided trecks on park territory, snorkelling, lectures on flora and fauna and marine life, and cultural demonstrations and activities; maps of the island's trails are available here.

Most visitors to St. John arrive for the day as accomodation on the island is limited. They leave the ferry and pile into tin-roofed safari buses which sea: up to 20 people, for a tour of the island: Bordeaux Mountain (the highest point on St. John, 1,272 ft. above sea level) which has wonderful views of the Atlantic, the Carribean and the nearby islands, Cor Bay, a swim at Trunk Bay, a look at the campsite at Cinnamon Bay, and finally back to the town square. North of the town is the world-famous **Caneel Bay**, : resort for the rich and famous created by Laurance Rockefeller on the site of an old estate (that on whic the planters gathered during the rebellion of 1733 t withstand the attack of the slaves). The resort is on a private peninsola of 170 acres in a beautiful park ful of tropical flowers: bougainvillea, poinsettia, jacaranda, hibiscus and coconut palms. The rooms are in bungalows, all near one of the seven private beaches. Other facilities are eleven tennis courts, several restaurants (two of them also open to non-Caneel Bay guests), a private ferry connecting Caneel Bay directly with St. Thomas and organised trips to the British Virgins.

ongoose Junction, a shopping centre good for both duty free opping and locally produced goods.

The ruins of sugar factory with its huge old windmill.

Following pages, Hawksnest Bay.

ONGOOSE JUNCTION

ongoose Junction is located near the National Park itors Centre in Cruz Bay and is a picturesque tle-like complex of studio shops with artisans at rk, arcades with boutiques, galleries, jewelry ps, bars, restaurants, and open areas with ches. It is good for pleasurable uncrowded duty- e shopping, and also for locally designed works of art, jewelry and clothing. The name was chosen as the mongoose is so common as to be almost a symbol of the island. It was brought to the islands in the 1800s to kill the cane rats but for this purpose was of little use as the rats, unlike mongooses, were able to climb trees and made their nests there and the mongooses hunted by day whereas the rats were out at night. They are, however, probably responsible for the fact that on St. John there are no snakes.

Another view of Hawksnest Bay.

THREE BEAUTIFUL NATIONALPARK BAYS:
HAWKSNEST BAY, TRUNK BAY AND CINNAMON BAY

The **Virgin Islands National Park** occupies 9,500 acres, largely donated by Laurance Rockefeller and the Jackson Hole Preserve Corporation; the land not included in the park is mainly the settled areas round Cruz Bay and Coral Bay.

The park, including the beaches and underwater, is maintained and protected by park officials who also enforce park rules, the aim of which is to limit the damage done by people. Near many of the park beaches boating is restricted, no water skiing, para-sailing or hang-gliding is allowed, fishing is permitted by rod or hand line and even then, away from swimming or snorkelling beaches.

Nothing must be broken, defaced or removed including marine plants and animals.

The park's **Visitors' Information Centre** in Cruz Bay organises many activities: nature walks along the forest trails, informative beach walks, bird-watching walks and snorkelling tours, all with knowledgeable and experienced guides. They also organise slide shows and lectures, cultural demonstrations and historic tours. The most spectacular guided trek is the Reef Bay Hike (usually 3 times a week), which is three mile downhill trail through forests, stopping for lunch at the mysterious petroglyphs. Of these carvings there is little known and experts are divided into those who believe them to be pre-Columbian, symbols from the days of the peaceful

Arawaks or the fierce cannibal Caribs, and those who believe them to have been carved by the African slaves. Just behind the beach at Reef Bay, hikers pass a restored steam-powered sugar mill, the last to be used on the island. The park boat meets them at Reef Bay.

The reef-fringed north-west shore of the island has the longest and most spectacular park beaches. Three of the most beautiful are **Hawksnest Bay, Trunk Bay,** and **Cinnamon Bay**.

Boats are not allowed to anchor in sweeping **Hawksnest Bay**, animals are not allowed, as on all park beaches, and there are no concessions. There are several beaches and snorkelling and swimming are excellent.

Nearby **Trunk Bay** is rated among the ten most beautiful beaches in the world and is the most popular beach with tourists from St. Thomas and those based on St. John. It was named after the "trunk-back" turtle, better known as the leatherback turtle, as it has no visible shell but a leathery skin in which the bones of the shell are buried. It is the largest living turtle and can attain up to 2 m in length, but as it used to be hunted for its oil, it is rarely seen now.

In Trunk Bay where visibility is excellent there is a 200 yd. long snorkelling trail, which can be reached from the beach and is ideal for novices. Informative signs indicate common coral formations and marine creatures.

Trunk Bay.

Two views of Cinnamon Bay

A giant kapok tree.
St. John's best known giant Kapok tree with its turkey-feet roots is o.
Cinnamon Beach; there are about 20 all together on the island.
Sometimes known as silk cotton, they can grow as high as 80 ft.

Cinnamon Bay, the next bay continuing east along the north coast is famous for its campsite which is situated just behind the beach. Run by the National Park Services, it was started in 1964 and is inexpensive and probably the most sought after accomodation in the West Indies (it must be booked a year in advance and no more than two weeks in a year may be spent there). The complex of 50 tents and 40 cottages provides all camping necessities: picnic table, charcoal grill, ice chest, water container, gas lamps, pots and pans, eating utensils and bed linen. Facilities offered are a restaurant, a mini-market, a fully-equipped water sports centre and even a little museum with island relics. Several interesting park trails start across the road from the bay and there is also a Park Information Centre based here in an old Danish warehouse at the west end of the beach. This is the setting, in the evening, for slide shows, informal talks and informative films about flora and fauna, marine life and the culture and history of the West indies. It is also the site of a living history demonstration: campers bring supplies and a cook prepares native breads and biscuits which are then cooked in the outdoor wood-burning oven. From the beach, park rangers give snorkel tours and snorkelling lessons.

The sugar factory.

The windmill .

THE RUINS OF THE ANNABERG SUGAR AND RUM FACTORY

The **Annaberg Plantation** ruins are situated on Leinster Bay, near Mary Point where legend has it that the rebel slaves of 1733 threw themselves down the red cliffs rather than face capture. The ruins of the sugar and rum factory with its huge old windmill (one of the largest in the Virgin Islands) can be visited either on a guided tour or else following the informative guide leaflet available which points out and provides interesting information on, among other things, the slave quarters, the mill outbuildings and the rum-making equipment.
On this site there are also regular cultural demonstrations illustrating subsistence living from 1900-35. Topics include tropical foods, medicinal plants, charcoal making, weaving, baking and terraced gardening.

The northernmost beach on Leinster Bay is the site of the National Park Service seashore walk as it is rocky and thus offers good conditions to study beach formation and inter-tidal flora and fauna. The coral flats near the shore make swimming impossible here. The walk along the coral strewn beach takes an hour and a half and includes a fascinating mangrove lagoon.

CORAL BAY AND THE EMMAUS MORAVIAN CHURCH

Coral Bay was St. John's main harbour in the days of slavery with almost as much commercial traffic as St. Thomas. Because of its safe harbour (larger even than that of Charlotte Amalie, and judged by Admiral Nelson to be the best in the Lesser Antilles) it was here, in 1716, that the Danish West India and Guinea Company first established its large Estate Carolina plantation (of which the sugar mill can be visited). In 1717 Fort Berg was built on a hill on the peninsula and it was the stage in 1733 for the first act of the slave insurrection.

The name Coral Bay comes, not as one would suppose from the coral reefs round the island, but from the Dutch word "kraal" meaning "corral" (as in cows) because before the Danish settled, early buccaneers kept their cows here and sold beef (particularly cured beef, "buccan") to other islands.

From **Coral Bay Overlook**, many of the neighbouring British Virgin Islands lining the Francis Drake Channel can be seen. From here you can gaze down on **Hurricane Hole**, a protected bay that sailors have used in stormy weather for centuries: the many indentations are lined with mangroves which protect the land from storms and also shelter ships anchored among them from roaring winds and the onslaught of huge waves.

The **Emmaus Moravian Church**, manse and village here in Coral Bay was founded during the second half of the eighteenth century as a mission (that is, both church and working plantation) the second on St. John after the Bethany Mission at Cruz Bay. The present church is an 1918 reconstruction of the original which was partially destroyed; the complex is one of the least altered in the West Indies and as such was entered into the National Register of Historic Places.

The next bay east of huge Coral Bay is **Salt Pond Bay** interesting as having one of the few remaining active salt ponds in the Virgin Islands, behind the beach. Here during the dry months when the water evaporates and the crystals form a crust, the salt is "picked".

The Emmaus Moravian Church seen from the bay.

Views of the church.

ST. CROIX

The island of **St. Croix** (pronounced Saint Croy) is the largest of the U.S. Virgin Islands, being about 20 miles long and 7 miles wide at its widest point. It has two main towns: Christiansted on the northern coast and Frederiksted on the western tip. It is not so mountainous as the other two and is probably not part of the same volcanic northern island mass. The island shows amazing geographic diversity: the southern coast is a coastal plain, then in the north west are Blue Mountain and Mount Eagle, both rising to above 1,000 ft. Also in the northwest is a rain forest with hanging vines and mahogany trees. The eastern end of the island, on the other hand, is arid, a virtual desert of sweeping grassland spotted with cacti. St. Croix was first inhabited by Indians who called it Ay-Ay. Remains of both the peaceful Arawaks and the fierce cannibalistic Caribs have been found and it is thought that the Arawak settlements preceeded those of the Caribs who came swarming north and killed or enslaved the Arawaks. In any case, when European settlers arrived in the early seventeenth century there were no Indians left on the island. The first hundred years of European settlement were very unstable with the English, Dutch, French and Spanish claiming, fighting over and buying and selling the island. For about fifteen years it was the property of the Knights of Malta who were responsible for its present name: Columbus had named it Santa Cruz (Holy Cross) which under the French knights became St. Croix. In 1733 the island was bought by the Danish West India and Guinea Company who systematically divided the land into 150 and 300 acre estates which were then sold at good rates to encourage settlement. Planters flocked in from other nearby islands, the majority of them English, Irish or Scots which explains why the language on St. Croix has always been English. By 1755 when the island became a Danish Crown Colony, there were some 375 plantations under cultivation with sugar, cotton, indigo and tobacco as main crops, and a population of over 10,000. The highest point in St. Croix's economical success was towards the end of the eighteenth century, then began a slow decline due to a variety of factors including the Danish Government's banning of the slave trade (1803), the freeing of slaves (1848), labour riots, fires, hurricanes, an earthquake, and the depression years. However St. Croix carried on producing both sugar and cotton right into this century. It now, unlike the other two islands, has two large industrial enterprises: the huge Hess Oil Refinery and the Virgin Islands Alumina Corporation and also continues rum production and cattle farming, all on the flat south coast near the airport.

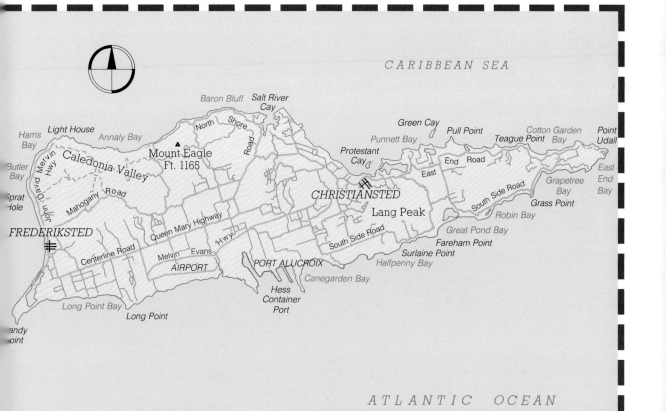

hristiansted and the yellow structure of Fort Christianvaern seen .om the harbour.

The battlements of Fort Christianvaern.

rotestant Cay.

CHRISTIANSTED

hristiansted, is the largest town on St. Croix, but espite this it has kept the appearance of a charming tle Caribbean harbour. It is situated on a natural arbour, centrally placed on the north coast, on what as the site of the French town Bassin. When the anes bought the island they changed the name to at of the then King of Denmark and planned the wn following the same scheme as many Danish anned towns of the eighteenth century: broad reets were arranged in a grid pattern, at right igles to one another and a large dock area was left r loading and unloading ships and the traffic this volved.

ost buildings in Christiansted are eighteenth or neteenth century Danish: cream coloured with red ofs and shady arcades and galleries. The cturesque old wharf area is so well preserved that has been designated a National Historic Site and is pervised by the U.S. Park Service which offers ily walking tours of the area.

ort Christianvaern was rebuilt on the site of the

French Fort Saint Jean, using hard yellow bricks transported as ballast in sailing ships. It was finished in 1749 and is a typical and well preserved example of Danish seventeenth and eighteenth century military architecture. It was used as a garrison until 1878 and then it became the police station and courthouse. Visitors can follow a self-guided tour through the powder magazine, dungeons, officers' kitchen, the soldiers' cells and battlements with cannons positioned all along them.

The harbour itself has a tricky entrance channel past the 2-mile Long Reef which protects this part of St. Croix's north shore and the waters are also shallow, so large ships avoid it and cruise ships dock at Frederiksted. In the middle of the harbour is **Protestant Cay** (pronounced "key") which, according to legend, was the burial grounds of non-Catholics when the French possessed the island, hence the name. It is now known for its beach, the closest to the town, and the resort situated on it, **Hotel on the Cay**.

The Scale House.

The Customs House

Government House

THE OLD SCALE HOUSE, AND THE DANISH CUSTOMS HOUSE

The **Old Scale House**, built in the mid 1800s, faces the waterfront on **Kings Wharf** and was where merchandise was inspected and weighed in order to set taxes and import duties. The old scales are still here, built into the floor and today this building houses the Visitors' Bureau which provides information, brochures and a free walking tour map. This wharf area was the focal point of the town when trade in sugar, cotton, rum and molasses was flourishing. Nearby is the old **Danish Customs House**, part of which dates back to 1751. It is now used for art exhibitions.

GOVERNMENT HOUSE

Government House on King Street is a huge and beautifully proportioned building with an external ceremonial staircase leading directly into the grand ballroom where important functions were held when Christiansted was the capital of the Danish West Indies and this was the headquarters and official residence of the Danish Governor-General. Originally it was built by a merchant in 1742 and was bought by the Danish Government in 1771. In the 1830s an adjoining house (built between 1794-7) in the side street was bought and added to it. It was badly damaged in a fire in 1936 and for the restoration Copenhagen contributed the 28 mirrors in the ballroom and the candelabra. It is still the headquarters for the St. Croix government offices. Across from Government House was the hardware store where Alexander Hamilton worked when he was thirteen. He was born on the British island of Nevis in 1755, but his mother was Cruzan and they returned to St. Croix. Hamilton lived and worked here until, with the finacial help of benefactors and friends who had noticed his outstanding intelligence he was able to go to study in Boston.

CHRISTIANSTED HARBOUR AND WHARF

A popular and well catered for boat trip from Christiansted is that to **Buck Island Marine Park**, situated east of Christiansted off the north coast, a trip of around six miles. In 1961 Buck Island was declared a National Park monument because of the spectacular coral reef which encircles it. The eastern end of the island is famous for its underwater snorkelling trail, one of the first in the Caribbean, with submerged notices providing information on marine life. There is also a scuba area with coral caves to explore. A choice of boats is always available, including glass-bottomed boats, and most offer a six-hour round trip, allowing snorkelling time, beach time and time to explore the island's flora and fauna following the National Park trail. There are over 60 different types of trees and more than 40 bird species including the brown pelican who nests here.

The historical waterfront hotel, Club Comanche's windmill replica which houses a honeymoon suite.

The Steeple Building

The Friedensthal Moravian Church

The wharf seen from the harbour.

THE STEEPLE BUILDING AND THE FRIEDENSTHAL MORAVIAN MISSION

The **Steeple Building** is situated on Company Street and was constructed in 1750-3 as the Lutheran Church of the Lord of Zebaoth (the Sabbath). The steeple was added in the 1790s. In 1831 the Lutherans abandonned it because it was in a poor state of repair and the building was successively used, with the necessary structural alterations, as a military bakery and storehouse, a hospital and a school. It now houses a small museum of island history including Arawak and Carib artifacts, a model of a sugar plantation illustrating sugar cane processing and a diorama of Christiansted in the early 1800s.

Across the road from the Steeple Building at the corner of Company and Church Streets is the large pink structure of the what was the **Danish West India and Guinea Company warehouse**. Built in 1749 it once contained provision stores, offices and living quarters round a courtyard which was used as a slave market.

Outside the historic centre and just beyond the cemetry, stands the **Moravian Mission of Friedensthal**, which is the name of the estate on which it stands. It was established during the middle of the eighteenth century after the pattern of the other missions already based on the other two Danish islands, and like them was both plantation and place of worship. The impressive masonry church with its portico on the north side was built in 1852.

ST. JOHN'S ANGLICAN CHURCH

St. John's Anglican Church is located at the beginning of Kings Street next to the cemetery and was constructed in 1849 replacing an earlier stone church of 1772. It still has much of its original woodwork inside.

The church mirrors the Virgin Islands interpretation of Gothic Revival perfectly, even though it has undergone various alterations over the years in order to meet the needs of an expanding Anglican congregation.

Façade and interior of St. John's Anglican Church.

Aerial view of Salt River Bay.

SALT RIVER BAY

alt River Bay, on the north coast of the island, was nce really the estuary of Salt River, which had its ource near Canaan and came down through Estate Concordia into Salt River Bay. Probably for this eason there have been various major settlements ere in the past. It is an important archaeological site nd the account left by Columbus 500 years ago of ne Indian villge he found here has been orroborated by digging this century which has rought to light artifacts and utensils which allow a artial reconstruction of the identity and life of these ndians (a collection is in the Steeple Building luseum). It is one of over 40 Indian sites on St. Croix nd one in which evidence of both the Arawaks and arlike Caribs has been found. Also at Salt River a ow of stone slabs with petroglyphs and pictograms as discovered.

n the seventeenth century the east bank of Salt River ay was government headquarters for the French nights of Malta who had been given St. Croix by Governor de Poincy, one of their leaders, and then Governor of the French West Indies. Their triangular earthwork fort, Fort Sàle, is still visible today on the west bank with their landing stage and customs house up river from the fort just off the present Northshore Road.

The French Governor, Chevalier du Bois, who arrived in 1659 built himself a little French chateau with towers at each end (one of which can still be seen) on what is now Estate Judith's Fancy, next to Salt River Bay.

Legend attributes to him the importation of the ancestors of the little white tailed deer which still live on the island for his park. The Knights of Malta were also, incidentally, responsible for burning all the forests and woodland because they believed them to be the cause of malaria, watching the fires for months from their ships. This probably had an effect on the plantation era, as the composted ash became richly fertile soil.

THE MANGROVE LAGOON AT SALT RIVER BAY

On the south west shore of Salt River Bay is the largest stand of mangroves on the island, and one of the largest in the U.S. Virgin Islands. Until recently the important roles that mangroves play in the marine environment was not completely understood and many stands were destroyed for development. Now the larger stands have "critical habitat" status and are protected by both local and federal legislation. Mangrove lagoons are the salt marshes of the tropics, where water from the land is filtered, the land is protected from the sea (mangrove lagoons are very safe anchorages) and a very important marine nursery and shore bird habitat is provided.

The three types of mangroves in the Salt River stand are red, white and black, each of which, though bearing the same name, has very different needs and characteristics; so much so that they tend to grow in distinct zones, separate from one another rather than mingling. The red mangrove is the mud-maker and the leader: it traps debris in its roots which in time decays to a rich dark mud. However the red mangrove itself prefers clear water and moves away from the mud (the floating roots germinate and at a certain stage of growth detach themselves from the parent tree; they can spend weeks floating around until they find a suitable sandy bottom where they can take hold and sprout). The black mangroves live on mud flats which are periodically flooded and the white live a little further in on harder saline soil. Both of these last trees exude excess salt from pores on their leaves.

alt River Bay.

National Historic Landmark recording the Columbus landing site.

THE COLUMBUS LANDING SITE

olumbus reached St. Croix, then called Ay-Ay by the native Indians, on November 14th 1493. He renamed it Santa Cruz after the Holy Cross and his eet stopped at the small estuary now called Salt ver Bay. Some men were sent ashore to look for esh water; they found a native village from which e Indians had fled leaving a few Arawak slaves ho they took captive. They then had an encounter ith some Carib Indians in a canoe who wounded o of Columbus' men, one mortally. Columbus med the spot "Cabo de Flechas" (Cape of the rrows). This spot is now much visited by tourists d picnickers. Salt River Bay itself has one of the ost popular diving sites on the island, the Salt River bmarine Canyon which is also the location of the **ydrolab Project**: a four-person underwater habitat 50ft. under in which groups of scientists live for a eek at a time studying marine biology.

...rambola Beach Resort on the north coast of St. Croix.

...at Hall, a historic hotel.

...RAMBOLA BEACH RESORTS
...ND SPRAT HALL

...rambola Beach Resorts on Davis Bay is situated in
...e of the greenest and lushest areas, on the north
...e of the island, about half way between
...ristiansted and Frederiksted.
...d-watching is popular here and the resort also
...ts one of the island's three golf courses.
...rat Hall is a historic Inn about 350 years old, where
...h caracteristic rooms in the style of the old
...nters and modern accomodations are available.
...rat Hall is situated on the west side of St. Croix
...ere the white sand beach is one of the most
...pular places for riders.

Views of the Fort at Frederiksted.

FREDERIKSTED

Frederiksted is a small picturesque town with an excellent deep sea harbour where cruise ships dock. The town centre, wide streets in a grid pattern was planned in the early 1750s by a Danish surveyor, and the Fort, intended to discourage smuggling to St. Eustatius, was finished in 1760. Fort and town were named after King Frederik V of Denmark. The low arcaded buildings we see now were nearly all rebuilt according to Victorian taste after the "fire-burn" of 1878 when much of the town was burnt leaving intact only the fire-resistant stone ground floors. Frederiksted never attained the importance intended for it, it was always a fraction of the size of Christiansted and was never much more than a convenient port for planters on the west side of the island.

Frederiksted was the stage for some important moments in the island's history. It was to Frederiksted that 8,000 slaves marched in 1848, demanding immediate freedom rather than the 12-year program of gradual freedom decided on by the Danish king, and threatening to riot and burn. The then Governor Von Scholten evaluated the risk and from the battlements of Fort Fredeiksted he read his famous proclamation: "All unfree in the Danish West Indies are from today free."

This was, however, only the start of problems on St. Croix and thirty years later, again in Frederiksted, after years of bad crops and a series of natural disasters, the field labourers rioted on the official contract-signing day spurred by tensions over labour regulations. Warehouses, shops and houses were looted and set on fire; most of the north-west part of Frederiksted was burned. Driven out of the town by troops from Christiansted, the rioters continued their destruction for five days, moving through the countryside burning sugar factories and greathouses. This uprising was known as the "fire-burn" of 1878.

It was after this that Frederiksted was rebuilt with all its Victorian decorative features. Today the restored fort houses a meeting hall and a museum specializing in the military history of the island, with pictorial display of the "fire-burn" and emancipation.

The pier seen from Strand Street.

Strand Street which runs along the waterfront.

Typical Frederiksted houses in the historic centre.

THE ARCHITECTURE OF FREDERIKSTED

Some common characteristics can be observed in Frederiksted architecture, many of which can also be seen in other towns in the ex-Danish West Indies. Buildings are usually no higher than two floors, ground and first, because of the danger of hurricanes and earthquakes. The ground floor was usually used as shop or workshop and the upper floor was the living quarters with an external staircase from the street to reach it.

The ground floor walls and the foundations had to be masonry because of the risk of fire; they were mostly thick rubble (limestone, broken brick, volcanic rock and coral). Bricks and limestone slabs were sometimes used but were much more costly materials as bricks were all imported and limestone

had to be cut by hand. They were usually used only when strength was needed, for columns, arches and vaulted ceilings. The rubble walls were plastered and sometimes this plaster was incised with lines to give it the appearance of cut stones.

The upper part of a building was often wood (it was this part of many buildings which was destroyed in the "fire-burn" of 1878). There are often shady galleries round this floor, sometimes extending over the pavement in front of the house, supported by masonry or wooden columns, providing cool arcades underneath. The attractive Victorian gingerbread trim which now characterises Frederiksted is mainly attached to the galleries and the eaves. There are also often ornate porches over the front door and the galleries have charming wooden balusters. The designs of this decorative woodwork vary charmingly from house to house.

A house on Kings Street.

The Catholic Church of St. Patrick.

THE HISTORIC BUILDINGS OF FREDERIKSTED

A free map and walking tour guide can be obtained at the Visitor's Bureau on the corner of Strand and Lagoon Streets near Fort Frederik. Some of the most interesting buildings are the **Old Customs House**, virtually opposite the pier, dating back to the end of the eighteenth century; then on the waterfront Strand Street, the **Lacy Victoria House** on the corner with Market Street, built in 1803 and restored after the fire, and the **Public Library**, on the corner with Queen Cross Street, again dating back to 1803. On King Cross Street is **Apothecary Hall**, the old chemist from the second half of the nineteenth century. **St. Paul's Anglican Church** from 1812 which has beautiful carpentry work inside and **St. Patrick's Roman Catholic Church** (1848) are both on Prince Street, as is the **Old Danish School**. The **Holy Trinity Lutheran Church**, built in 1792 (the cupola is a later addition) is between New Street and Hill Street and nearby is the **Midlands Moravian Church and Manse in Friedensfeld**, 1-6 Hospital Street, the last of the three main Moravian centres on St. Croix. The original church was constructed in 1810 and this one was erected in the 1850s; it has some very impressive carpentry work. Lastly, on Market Street is the market place which has been on the same site since 1751.

For divers, another attraction in Frederiksted is the pier, which is one of the leading pier dive sites in the Caribbean. The pilings have become overgrown with brightly coloured encrusting corals and sponges and it provides a habitat for many species of fish, even some rare ones, and for the famous Frederiksted pier sea-horses which can only be seen on night dives.

THE ST. GEORGE VILLAGE BOTANICAL GARDENS

The St. George Village Botanical Gardens are situated on the Estate St. Georges and Sallys Fancy, east of Frederiksted, just off the Queen Mary Highway. It is a 16-acre garden with over 800 well-labelled species of exotic tropical plants, flowers and trees, planted in a beautiful setting, around the crumbling stone ruins of a nineteenth century sugar plantation. The ruins of the village and rum factory include workers' homes, the manager's house, an oven, a stone dam, a blacksmith's shop and the foundations of a watermill.

Views of the St. George Botanical Gardens.

Above, a view of a typical greathouse, now used for concerts and other cultural events.

The windmill at Whim

Following pages and bottom right, views of St. Croix

ESTATE WHIM PLANTATION MUSEUM

Estate Whim Plantation Museum, situated southwest of Frederiksted off the Concordia Road, is a monument to the island's age of prosperity, in the second half of the eighteenth century. Then the land was divided into well over 300 estates, the owners of which gave them the poetic names by which they are still known: All-for-the-Better, Contentment, Wheel of Fortune, Catherine's Rest, Work and Rest, Betzy's Jewell, Bonne Esperance, Lower Love, Upper Love, and so on. Even now, the imposing hill-top ruins of sugar mills and greathouses are one of the most characteristic sights on St. Croix.
Whim Estate dates back to 1751, in 1764 it was given the name John's Rest when the owner John Delaney was buried there. It is unknown who built the greathouse but it is thought probable that it was built by MacEvoy, Jr. who inherited it in 1794. The name was changed to Whim in 1803.
The greathouse, in neo-Classic European style with curved ends and a "moat" provides an idea of life on St. Croix when plantation owners were wealthy and had a life-style very much like that of rich Europeans. It is furnished with period antiques: fine furniture, silver and china either donated by Denmark or provided by old Crucian families.
Aspects of life in the eighteenth and nineteenth centuries are recreated with various exhibits. "Crucian Craftsmen" is dedicated to everyday craftsmen of the past, for example the blacksmith, the wheelwright, the carpenter and the cooper. A woodworking workshop has been recreated and holds demonstrations and the fixtures of an eighteenth century apothecary shop are on display. A huge stone windmill and mule-mill have also been fully restored and mid-nineteenth century Scottish steam engines for crushing and distilling can be seen.

Two views of golf courses.

...ight, Buccaneer Golf Course.

GOLF ON ST. CROIX

...here are three golf courses on St. Croix: two 18-
...ole championship courses at **Carambola Resort**
...nd **The Buccaneer**, and a 9-hole course at **The
...eef**. Carambola Resort is situated north-west, on
...e coast; its challenging golf course is on a terrain
...otted with ponds and lakes and the remains of old
...ugar mills. It was designed by Robert Trent Jones.
...he Buccaneer is near Christiansted and its course
...as designed by Bob Joyce. Lessons and
...urnaments can be arranged by the resident pro.
...oth of these courses offer well equipped pro
...ops, a pro, a practice putting green and a
...riving range. The 9-hole Reef golf course is at
...ague Bay on the east point of St. Croix.

INDEX